POEMS
FROM THE
Heart

POEMS
FROM THE
Heart

ROBIN PENMAN SMITH

POEMS FROM THE HEART

iUniverse books may be ordered through booksellers or by contacting:

iUniverse
1663 Liberty Drive
Bloomington, IN 47403
www.iuniverse.com
1-800-Authors (1-800-288-4677)

ISBN: 978-1-5320-9274-9 (sc)
ISBN: 978-1-5320-9298-5 (e)

Library of Congress Control Number: 2020900639

Print information available on the last page.

iUniverse rev. date: 01/14/2020

CONTENTS

LOVE POEMS

NATURE POEMS

LET ME TELL YOU A STORY: THE ODDITIES

FAITH AND CONTEMPLATION

For Diana, my wife and best friend

LOVE POEMS

WHEN LOVE IS KNOWN

When love is known and passion grows
Between a man and his sweet rose,
The heavens above and the earth beneath
To both lovers do great joy bequeath,
But the ways of a man and maid no-one knows.

Love is as mysterious as the wind that blows
And those who love not, should not suppose
That they understand how love flows
When love is known.

For love is mysterious as the wind that blows
And love itself has highs and lows.
And must be nurtured, for time is a thief
That must be countered by firm belief
In the God of love who true love bestows
When love is known.

BREAD AND BUTTER LOVES

Bread and butter loves above all other loves,
The stuff of every day give and take,
Outlast the show and flash of lesser loves,
The shallow loves that make hearts bend and break.

Fond affection, the first of all true loves,
The love of brother for brother which none can fake,
Sweet Eros, the fuel of all romantic loves,
God's pure love from Him who died for our sake.

All true loves in an indissoluble bond
Mingle together in the human heart,
Loves given, loves to which our hearts respond,
Are melded together with sublime art,
In every day bread and butter love
All true loves flow down freely from above.

DESIRE AND FULLFILMENT

There is sweet delight hidden in desire.
There is yearning strong each lover knows.
Too easy conquest disappointment sews.
There is yearning that sets the heart on fire,
There is wooing that flows from desire
Enflaming the heart as each lover knows.
It reveals the heart and all its nature shows
Fanning the bright flames of the heart on fire.
Such yearnings and such wooing bear fruition
When both lover and beloved know themselves
As whole, yet each the other gladly serves
Without dissembling or diminution.
Blessed the lovers who belong each to other
And covenant to love one another.

ELLE EST BELL

Elle est belle
Ce bon ami,
cette femme mienne.
Ensemble, nous parlons,
nous rions,
nous pleurons,
et nous avons confiance
dans le Dieu qui nous aime.

She is beautiful
This good friend,
this wife of mine.
Together we speak,
we laugh,
we cry,
and we trust
in the God who loves us.

ON THE THEOLOGY OF ROMANTIC LOVE

Brightly shines the morning light my own true love,
The world is freshening with the morning dew.
By the magnolia softly coos the dove,
When you're with me my love, and I'm with you.
All God's gracious gifts flow from heaven above,
Blessings in abundance, love gifts not too few,
Our hearts are open and our hearts are true.
God's love in us is an ever flowing love,
Flowing from the tumultuous love of God,
From Father, Son and Holy Spirit, our God,
A torrent of God's love in us enfleshed.
Side by side and hand in hand with Him we walk,
In the cool of the evening we three talk.

FIVE PASSIONS SONGS

I
Love is a flame poem.
Its heat sparkles in our hearts.
Brightly leaps its words.

II
Fire embers fanned
By bold, word spat memories,
Quick fierce angry strokes.

III
Hallelujah love!
God fire in your brilliant eyes.
Passion burns our dross.

IV
Bite deep, jab, counter.
Mouth wounds with realistic pain.
Eyes in sorrow mist.

V
Flash fire love again,
Flame rage, love rage, make us one.
Souls meld in sharing.

AT THE VAN GOGH MUSEUM IN AMSTERDAM

Along the beach wavelets lap the pebbled shore,
White gulls rise clamouring in the morning air.
When we're together all is bright and fair.
Who could ask, my dear, for anything more?
Vincent's boats rest upon the sandy shore,
Mediterranean light in glowing air,
Clear radiance, brilliance de la Mer.
Gazing, we stand upon a marble floor
Our eyes glancing from picture to picture;
The yellow house sits on a corner at Arles,
Yellow bed, yellow chairs, simple furniture;
A pink peach tree, and a wheatfield all gnarls.
All truth and beauty flow from God above
Poured forth in our hearts from the God of love.

DESIRE AND FULFILLMENT

There is a delight hidden in desire.
There is a yearning strong each lover knows.
Too easy conquest disappointment sews.
There is a yearning that sets the heart afire.
There is a wooing that flows from desire
That enflames the heart as each lover knows,
That reveals the heart and all its nature shows
Fanning the bright flames of the heart on fire.
Such yearnings and wooing bear fruition
When each lover and beloved know themselves
As whole, yet each the other gladly serves
Without dissembling or diminution.
Blessed the lovers who belong to each other
And covenant to love one another.

INDISSOLUBLE HEAVENLY LOVE

There is a gift given to humankind
In indissoluble heavenly love
Poured in our hearts from God above.
Some will receive it, but some are blind
And they are lost; while others with joy are entwined.
Love has come and the voice of the turtledove
Is heard in the land singing of love,
Of beauty, of truth, and of joy unconfined.
Arise my true love and come away
To the meadows and woods and the dells,
With the glad ringing of interior bells
In the hearts where the King of Love holds His sway.
For love is meant to be lived, not denied,
For by love alone is our God glorified.

AUTUMN WINDS

When autumn winds come knocking at my door
They carry with them crispness in the air,
And all the beauty of the leaves so fair
Tell the inner beauty of she whom I adore.
In autumn love's true springtime sings once more
But sings with a richness beyond compare
Taught by our tears and things we had to bear.
Autumn's bounteous harvest of glad amour
Is richer far than springtime's budding love,
And glows with the warmth of a golden light
That flows from the heart of heaven above,
For autumn's love is fraught with Love's delight.
I would not trade this love for springtime love.
Early love can't compare with autumn bright.

AFTER ALL THESE YEARS

After all these years
In times of joy
And times of tears,
My love abides for you,
You are my gift from God, my counterpart
As I am a gift and counterpart of you,
We rejoice in our Creator's art
That has crafted us together
In the image of Himself, together,
Male and female, bound together,
Living through all kinds of weather,
Of clouds and storms and sunny skies,
Marked by trials and joyous cries.
I would not have it any other
Than the precious gift of one another.

AN ANNIVERSARY

When you walk with the one you love
        for fifty years and more
A lifetime is locked in the memory's store,
Some difficult things that you shared before
And the tender things you shared
        with the one whom you adore.
Looking back over all the passing years
At all the joys and all the fears
You recognize that underneath you both
        are the everlasting arms,
That have carried you, and kept you both
        from everlasting harms.
Such love, long lived, is a precious thing
That makes my humble heart dance and sing.

TOUCH

I reach out my hand to touch her.
It is not a matter of sensuality
But merely, "I am here, and you are here."
Love is not always a matter of words,
But of a thousand light touches.
This is also true of the love of God,
For touching is not only physical
But an exchange from heart to heart.

LOVE IS A TOUGH AND TENDER THING

Love is a tough and tender thing
Nurtured in the fire of experience,
Only then can the true heart sing
And of God's grace give evidence.
As the years pass solemnly by
With all their joys and woes
Know this, know this, I cry,
That you are loved by your Lord and I
He, your first true Lover, loves you,
As do I, who run this race with you.
Before you loved me, or I loved you
He loved us both and called your name
He died to demonstrate His love for you
And rose to set our hearts aflame.

ON THE ORIENT EXPRESS

In the Railway Station
Oriental sumptuousness,
Travelers and Peddlers.

We traveled once, Diana and I,
From Venice to Zurich
By Overnight Express,
Cabinette, silver service,
And linen table clothes.
Curried chicken and white rice
And the Alps gliding
Majestically by.

"Mr. Ratchett has been frontally stabbed,
Twelve times."
But not on our train.

On our train, love,
And precious memories;
Along the canal in Venice
Roasted sparrow and fried sardines,
As the gondolas glide swiftly by.
And in Zurich an Oompah Band
In the hotel basement,
And in a small estaminet
Along the street,
Champignons sur du pain grille.

While Wretched Ratchett
Is wretchedly murdered
By twelve good men and true.

But that was on another train,
And all the while we walked
Hand in hand
Along the streets of Zurich.

PARLE DOUCEMENT

Parle doucement
Speak softly

Speak softly and no one will hear,
We live our love, just the two of us
Nobody knows the truth we feel, it is ours alone,
Not even the sky that's watching us from above

Je veux rester à vos côtés,
Mon amour, toujours.
I want to stay by your side,
My love, always.

Speak softly, and come closer to me,
I want to feel my eyes inside of you,
And your loving eyes within me.
Nobody knows the truth we feel.

Je veux rester à vos côtés,
Mon amour, toujours.
I want to stay by your side,
You are my love, always.

Speak softly, and come closer to me,
I want to feel my eyes inside of you,
And your loving eyes within me.
Nobody knows the truth we feel.

Le grand cadeau de l'amour
Est une grâce de Dieu
Cela dure pour toujours.
This great gift of love
Is a grace of God
That endures for ever.

THE MEETING OF OUR EYES

Across a crowded room
By grace, a gift, a glance,
The meeting of our eyes,
Love is a wonderful thing!
There's nothing quite as rare
As loving hearts beyond compare.
All the world spins 'round
But we have a stable place
For our love holds firm
In the loving heart of God.

THERE IS A LOVELESS COLD

There is a loveless cold that makes
The breath quiver, the bones ache.
It is not a mere state of mind
But a pain that makes the soul quake.

Love is a gift of God so kind,
And very often you and I will find
That God's love is most truly given
Through us, in this world, to one another.

For God's love to fully bloom
Open your hearts and make room,
Let God's love be the leaven
That heals our hearts and conquers pride.

As brother gives to brother,
And to sister, father, and mother
In sweet communion side by side
Where we dwell, this side of heaven.

NATURE POEMS

IN THE EARLY DAWN

In early dawn
Before the rising of the sun
Faint silver light glows
Upon the rolling sea
Illuminating its waves.
Then golden light rises
Along the eastern horizon
And the sun leaps up to follow
Its appointed course
At the beginning of the day.

REFLECTED LIGHT

Early in the morning we rose in the chilly air
to behold the nature of God in the lunar eclipse.
So may all the enemies of righteousness
Be eclipsed by the shadow of God's kingdom.
But give heed to this, and understand,
Both the earth and its moon have no light
Of their own, but reflect the light of the sun.
Give heed to this all you rulers of the earth!
You have no light of your own
But only the light that flows from the Truth.
If the light that is in you is darkness
Woe to all those who follow you.

CLOUDY DAY

Cloudy day
Rainy day
No place to play
Inside or outside,
It's nature's way.
It's springtime,
Not winter time.
Even on a cloudy day
There is sunshine
Beneath the clouds.
Springtime blossoms
Are on the boughs
Tomorrow is another day.

EVER SINCE MID-SUMMER

Ever since mid-summer
The days are getting shorter,
Now by mid-September
The tired sun rises later
And runs its shortening course
Sinking wearily in the West.
The heavy apples on the trees,
The swelling melons in the garden,
The golden grain in the fields,
All things wait their harvest time.
Soon the leaves will wither
As winter pushes Fall before it.

CITY SUMMER NIGHT

In the late night hours
I rise to walk the sleepy streets
Beneath the silvered moon.
Summer air is soft and warm.
Little breezes lift the willow fronds.
City sounds, distant, muted,
Traffic hum, siren's cry,
Dim crescendo of a rising jet,
Cat's cry and cricket's chirp,
And quick patter of a rabbit
Running through the shrubs.
Car door slams, voices jangle.
Through an open door I hear
Westminster chime and chime again,
Two o'clock, two o'clock,
The night rolls on.

DOWN THE HILL AND AROUND THE BEND

Down hill and around the bend
The country road winds on and on.
Along its sunlit path I wend
Beneath the spreading oaks and pines.
A fragrance fills the air,
A freshness beyond compare,
And the melodies of bird song
Echoes all around.

MAPLE SUGAR TIME

How I miss the soft quietness
that follows a deep snow fall,
the crispness of the air,
the crunch of snow under my feet;
the long slow spring
as the sun warms and thaws the earth.
The maple sap begins to flow
and we tap the trees,
boiling down the sap.
Early Spring is maple sugar time.

FOG

Milk bottle fog,
  opaque glass
  cloaks wisps of grass.
Treble monotone
bass and baritone
    lonely voices harp.
        "My rocks are sharp.
        All life is dear.
        No channel here."
    On still brine
    no sun will shine.
Milk bottle fog.

GAILY I FOLLOW AFTER

Beneath the leafy forest green
I walk through hidden paths unseen.
Among the beech and yellow birch
I pursue my relentless search
Looking for the white-tailed deer.
Roaming far and searching near,
Among sweet fern and rhodora
Painted trillium, and gay forest flora,
Pink lady-slipper and wild cherry
And the pink mayflower merry
Were I to find the white-tailed deer
By roaming far and searching near,
Would I hinder its joyful flight,
Or merely follow the merry sight?

IN THE GARDEN WHERE
I LOVE TO GO

In the garden where I love to go
I see the hollyhocks all planted in a row,
Peach and apple blossom, hyacinth and golden bell,
The Lily of the Valley, the greater celandine and daffodil,
Nothing can compare with God's great beauty rare.
In this wild profusion of His glory, a sight beyond compare,
Come walk with me a little, while the gentle breezes blow,
And share with me the beauty of His garden here below.

MORNING THUNDER

How lovely is the morning
When the thunder rolls across the skies
When God's melodies keep time
With his heavenly drums
And the rain falls softly all around.

SUNLIGHT MOONLIGHT

Sunlight, moonlight,
In all His glorious forms
Light of the world,
Light of my life,
Rising in the east
Setting only to rise again.
Light on moonlit waters,
Light on sunny meadows,
Light in the darkness,
Of the world,
Shine upon me.
Peace I give you,
Not as the world gives,
Give I you.
Let not your heart be troubled,
Neither let it be afraid.

THE RAIN CAME
THUNDERING DOWN

When I was very young and it was night
the rain came thundering down the inky sky,
pounding out its merry melody
on the tin roof of Mary Dealey's cottage;

A sturdy noble rain hammering on the roof,
drumming out its fearful marching sound,
a military marching rain, roaring,
echoing in the one room cabin.

From that night on I have loved the rain,
all the rain, the hammering rain, the spluttering rain,
the wind driven rain pounding on the ground,
and the little gentle drizzle falling all around.

The falling rain washes all the earth,
washes grass and leaves, flowers and trees,
washes little rocks and mighty boulders,
washes clean the very air we breathe.

O ye wind and rain; bless ye the Lord;
O ye cabins with tin roofs; bless ye the Lord;
O ye grass and leaves; bless ye the Lord;
O ye flowers and trees, bless ye the Lord;
O ye little rocks and boulders, bless ye the Lord;

O my joyful rain washed soul; bless ye the Lord;
Praise Him and magnify Him forever.

STORMY WEATHER

How the winds do blow
Whipping the branches of the trees
Scattering the leaves
Scooping up dust and dirt
And lashing it against
The cottage walls.
Then suddenly, not a sound,
Not a whisper, not a breeze,
Not a time to set your heart at ease.
The wind rises again
And starts to blow,
Whipping the branches of the trees,
Scattering the leaves,
Scooping up dust and dirt
To throw against
New cottage walls.
Now pass on, pass on.
Blow gentle winds blow
Blow away the clouds and rain
Bring sunshine to the land again.

UPON A STARRY NIGHT

How often in the midnight hours
I have risen in the dark,
when no flame was seen, no, not one spark.
In the dark I have walked the winding halls,
one hand upon the walls, out through the portals
and stood upon the gently sloping lawn.

The sky was bright
with a myriad, myriad, starry lights
upon the overarching vault, and
each reflected in the pool below.

Zephyr breezes stirred the waters,
the lilies danced, and
dancing upon the broad lily leaves
danced other lights,
not starry lights, but faery lights.

As I drew near their slender sylvan forms
I did perceive though unperceived.
Closer stepped I cautiously
but perceiving me each turned and courteously did bow,
then vanished westward from my sight
leaving naught behind but the tintinnabulation
of their crystal laughter chiming in the air.

As I stood listening upon the lawn,
the eastern sky began to lighten
and the strong Sun rose mightily to warm the earth.
The morning air was filled with birdsong;
a thousand, thousand, meadow larks

singing praise to their Creator,
and one old jackdaw croaked his delight;
yet mingled through the birdsong,
chiming faery laughter could be heard.

THE WIND

The wind frets along the edge of the roof
heavy handed, clumsy, batting at shingles,
baffled by their resistance,
with mindless persistence
tugging, pushing, pulling
in a stolid stupid sort of way.
It has played the game for hours
having nothing better to do.

THE FRESHENING BREEZE

Often in my mind I walk
In the sunshine and shadows
Of a New England woods,
Along a ferny pathway beneath
The towering pine and stately elm
Where the summer sunshine
And the shadows gently ripple,
As softly a freshening breeze
Blows through the reaching trees.

THE WINDS DO BLOW

The winds do blow and bring the snow
That covers all the land below.
And up above the sky is drear,
No harbinger of welcome cheer.
But in my heart the fire burns bright
It is a warm and merry sight.
Life's what you choose to make of it
Whether dark, or by Grace, sunlit.

BITTER BLOWS THE WIND

Bitter blows the wind
Across the meadow grasses.
The first breath of fall
Dimming summer sun,
Harbinger of winter death.
Time and all things pass.

DRIVING IN THE FOG

One morning
We drove to God
In a heavy fog
The shadow lands
Pressing upon us.
The encroaching spell,
An enchantment
Of wickedness,
Was pressing upon us.
A prayer driven wind
Scattered the fog
Leaving the bare bones
Of the land visible to sight.
Pray for the travelers
Who pray for the fog
To begin once more
For they do not want
Their sins to be seen.
Lord have mercy upon us.
Lord have mercy upon them.
Lord have mercy upon us,
And let your light shine.

THE WIND SINGS

The wind sings
through meadow grasses
whispers dry leaves
along wooded edges
raps broken branches
on bare trunks
rap tap
it plays a myriad melodies
thrumming wires
clanging trash lids
down deep fenced alleys
kicking cans
slamming doors
battering eaves
stealing small boy's caps
sending them
shrieking
laughing
down city streets.
The Wind sings.

SEA WINDS

Like a creaking door
Marsh hens cheep among the reeds.
Along the shore road
The sea winds blow the salt hay
Gently rippling its green gold

THE NOR'EASTER

The nor'easter blows
Its cool wind across the land.
Fall in New England.

THE RAW WINDS

When the raw wind blows,
And the cold frost nips your nose,
Winter days have come.

How cold the wind blows
It's chill nearly froze my nose.
January woes.

TELL ME, WHAT COLOUR IS THE SKY?

What is the colour of the sky on a crisp winter morning
When the grass is dead and the birds have fled,
And the blue bottle fly lies feet up on the windowsill?
What is the sound of the city on a winter night
When the wind is whispering through the leafless branches?
Tell me if you know. Tell me if you know.
I long to hear the stories of the quick and the dead
But tell them now, don't wait until you are dead.

THE SEASONS

The wind doth blow
And snowflakes fall
Along the garden path.
Come Winter, Spring,
Summer, Fall,
Each season follows
One after the other.
That why the buds
Are followed by the blossoms
And the blossoms
Are followed by the fruit
And winter prepares
For the coming of spring.
Every living being,
Yes, even you and me,
All have our seasons
Spring, Summer,
Fall and Winter,
Until we stand before
Our Heavenly King.

WITH THE RISING SUN

With the rising sun
All the singing birds,
Soaring in the sky,
Are praising God on high.
Praising in the early morn,
The King of kings
And Lord of lords.

FISH SCRAPS

We sit by the sea with the angry waves
Roaring and crashing against the rocky shore,
And the gulls swooping and shrieking overhead,
Fighting over rotting bait and fish scraps.
The clouds are scuttling across the blue sky
Like crabs scuttling across the barren rock,
Driven by a clear and freshening wind
Across the sky, cleaning the air and the mind.

'TIS OF THE ROSE I BEG HER PARDON

Of all the flowers in the garden,
'Tis of the Rose I beg her pardon.
The daffodil springs only in the spring
Even though she is a lovely thing.
The Rose blooms summer, spring, and fall,
Border shrub, garden bush, or climbing tall.
Reds and whites, pink and palest yellow
Bold and striking, or colours mellow.
Chrysanthemum will make you sneeze,
Like Ragweed borne upon the breeze.
But fragrant Rose with perfume pure
Sends for its message a sweet allure,
That bids me pluck it long before
The bloom is off the Rose that I adore.

LET ME TELL YOU A STORY: THE ODDITIES

I'M A LITTLE PORKER

I'm a little porky porker
A melodious little snorker
A charming piggy wiggy
Dancing my own little jiggy
Hopping up and down
In my silken gown.
Why not take a chance
And join my little dance?
If that doesn't tickle you
Do the thing that pleases you
And let me do the little thing
That makes my little heart sing.

A POEM FROM MY CAT

I reject the smelly food you bring,
and I killed that little squeaky thing.
Please don't bother me with silly talks
And I defy you to keep clean my litter box.
If you try to nap, I'll sit on your chest and stare
and I'll wake you up by chewing on your hair.
Serve me quickly when I yowl. That will do!
Enjoy this mouse I killed for you.

AT THE CATHEDRAL

At the Cathedral
The Choir rose to masticate a Psalm
And all the while the Organist
Danced against them
With all his fingers and his toes.

AN ODE TO BACON

As beautiful the romping pig
More glorious is the bacon,
Oh, bacon unexcelled!
Pork chops are mighty fine,
And so is whole roast pork
Beloved for the crackling.
But what if, more glorious
I had a whole pignanimous
Plate of bacon, bacon, bacon,
So much bacon that I could not
Begrudge a piece of bacon
To share with a friend of mine.
Oh, bacon, streaky bacon,
You are supernuminous,
Oh bacon, bacon, bacon.

I'M THE BIG DOG

I'm the big dog, I'm the boss now,
Old boss man didn't do it right
But I know how to fix it now
I can do it, he didn't do it right
I'm on the job. Now I'm the man,
Whatever it is I can, I can, I can.
Every little thing must go through me
Because I'm large and I'm in charge,
I'm the big dog and I'm in charge,
I'm the fixer and soon you'll see
Everything will soon be better now
'Cause I'm the man, I can, I can.

DAN, DAN, THE OLD PYPER'S SON

Dan, Dan, the old pyper's son,
Whose brother stole a pig and away he run,
Dan beat his drum as loud as he can
Bam, bam, bamity bam, bamity bam bam
Dan beat his drum and had lots 'o fun
Too bad he had no sense of rhythom
Bam bam bamity bam, bam bamity clunk
So nobody could march to the sound of his drum.

BOOM

Boom chicka boom
Boom chicka boom boom
Sometimes I wake in the middle of the night
Boom chicka boom
Boom chicka boom boom
Some times I wake with pain
Sometimes with imaginary fright
Boom chicka boom
Boom chicka boom boom
Asprin for the boom chicka pain,
The God who loves me for the fright.
I will love thee, O Lord my might
Boom boom chicka boom
Boom chicka boom boom boom

[Boom chicka boom with imaginary fright?
Not really, just needed a boom chicka rhyme
Boom chicka boom boom.
Well, what do you expect?

DANCE

Dance lightly
On the moonbeams
Far up into the sky.
Dance with the angels
Join their jubilant cry .
Quick step, quick step,
On the moonbeams
Far up into the sky.
Dance with the angels,
The moon beams,
And I.

HOT LOVE

Hot love can be tricksy
If love alone is your guide,
For love that is all passion
Needs wisdom, not more fire.
Hot love has no brains
Its flames can burn
Both the hot lover
And the object of his desire.

I'M A COW

I'm a cow
Jump the moon
Do it soon
Take a bow
Have a dream
Don't say No
Climb a ridge
Build a bridge
Up we go
Don't stay below
Have a dream
Don't say No

IN THE BATHROOM MIRROR

We have a mirror
Let's be quite clear
It is a cheap mirror
Full length
On the bathroom door.
We bought it
At the Dollar Store,
But again
Let's be quite clear,
It's a foul mirror,
It tells tremendous lies,
It warps and bends,
Adding pounds and age.
It lies, and laughs at me.

LET ME BE YOUR AVUNCULAR

Our avuncular uncle
A carbuncular caruncular,
A wattle on the surface of life,
Appears furunclar only
Once a year on Boxing Day
At family celebrations,
A diminutive homuncular
Seeking to remembered
Interpeduncular in the
Family Will and Testament.
But nobody remembers him,
He is only subpeduncular,
And he is not at all relative.

A rough interpretation:

Our uncly uncle
A pimply pimple
A wattle on the surface of life
Appears like a boil
Once a year on Boxing Day
At family celebrations
A diminutive dwarf
Seeking to be remembered
Intelligently in the
Family Will and Testament.
But nobody remembers him,
He is only a lesser thought
And not at all relative.

LIAR, LIAR, SINGING IN THE CHOIR

Liar, liar, singing in the choir
Singing tenor, singing bass,
Soprano or alto, you're still a liar
Hiding behind your smiling face.
Politics is an exciting game
When one is seeking fame.
Shaking fists and shouting
You're a bigot, you're a nothing
Vote for me
I'm an honest man,
I'm and honest woman,
Catch me if you can.

LORD EDGEWARE DIES

Sly Agatha Christie
Loves to tell a story,
Lord Edgeware Dies.
In meeting Lord Edgeware
We soon discover that
He is a brute of a man
And deserves to die.
Nonetheless his death
Is only a pretext to reveal
The wisdom of Hercule Poirot.

MIDSOMER MURDERS

Midsomer County
Is not a good place to live,
But a good place to die
On any day of the week,
Or on any given night.

If we won a vacation trip
Would we really want to go?
I mean, every time we visit
Some poor bloke is snuffed
Even though all he wanted
Was a proper cup of tea
And fish and chips for lunch.

Oh, oh, here comes Barnaby
Where were you at nine p.m.
On Wednesday night last?
Is this the only murder
On this mysterious night?
No? One, two, three and more.

MURDER IN THE NIGHT

Murder in the night
On the Orient Express,
"Ce n'est rien, Je me suis trompé".
It is nothing. I am wrong.
Or did he say,
"C'etait un cauchemaur?"
It was a nightmare.

The nightmare is Ratchett himself,
The baby killer Cassetti.
Mr. Beddoes says of him,
"Put a sewer rat in a suit,
It is still a sewer rat."
Cassetti is deservedly murdered.
"Bien, Monseiur!"

Sometimes justice is not simple, and
Sometimes the law is not justice,
But how does one decide, and
Just who makes the decision?
Eh bien, la vie est compliquée,
et est donc la mort.
Ah well, life is complicated
And so is death.

OH NOBLE BEAN

Oh Noble Bean
Wakey, wakey,
Drink three mugs
And you'll be shakey.

OH TO BE IN ENGLAND

Oh to be in England
Any time of year,
And whoever wakes in England
Sees upon the kitchen table
An English breakfast, a cup of tea;
And in the garden a meadow lark
Singing on the orchard bough
In England—now!
-apologies to Robert Browning

REMEMBERING THE PAST

Remembering the Past
Once when I was very young
I feared the good songs had all been sung.
But now that I am past my prime
And have wandered down through time
I see the true value of the fading past
And ponder over the songs that last.
And this I know, this alone is sure,
The things that longest last
Are the things that are most pure.

HEAD AND SHOULDERS

Head and shoulders, knees and toes,
Growing older has its woes.
Aches and pains and gaining weight
Many older folk share this fate.

OLD HANDS, YOUNG HANDS

By circle round,
Old hands tough,
Young hands rough
Join gently round.
An old saint sways,
And smiles seraphically
With glowing marbled eyes.
Round and round
Hands meld men,
Hands meld God.

ONE TWO THREE FOUR

One two three four
What do we adore?
Sweet potato swill,
Sweet potato swill,
And rolling in the mud.
What do we adore?
Sweet potato swill
And rolling in the mud.

POOR OLD AUNT JANE

There she is
In a desperate bid
Hoping to create the illusion
That she's still young.
Tight torn jeans, tight top,
Affecting a bouncing stride.
But it's not working!
The process of aging
Is like a bulldozer
Sweeping everything before it.
I wonder what she will look
Like in the casket
When the undertaker dresses her?
"Oh, that's not my aunt Jane,
Aunt Jane was always so young!"
Poor old aunt Jane.

PORTALS

I passed through the door
Scattering the memory
Of my intention.
I stood in the empty room
Pondering the reason why?
Nothing came to mind?
I passed once more through the door
Tracing back my steps
Looking blankly around me.
Doors erase memory.

PRINCESS SPRING WINTER FALL

Boom tiddy boom. Boom tiddy boom.
Princess Winter Spring Summer Fall
Had no common sense at all
She never knew, what to wear
Whether to Church, or to the fair.
But in truth, she didn't really care
So wherever she went, she had ball.
Boom tiddy boom. Boom tiddy boom. Hot-CHA!
[A note to Grammarians:
I put commas, where I want 'em,
'Cause Princess Winnie is a friend of mine.
Boom tiddy boom, Hot CHA!]

PUFF

Puff, Puff, Puff
Self-anointed dragon lady,
True enough your skin is green,
And your fangs are yellow and obscene,
But you are not really all that scary
You only think you are.

A RIGHT PROPER PIG

I'm a right proper pig
I won't wear me wig
When I'm dancing a jig
And I don't give a fig.
So there!
[*Le Cochon Danseur, a French Silent Film 1906*]

SHE WIGGLES AND SHE JIGGLES

She wiggles and she jiggles
Strutting her plumptous stuff,
Looka me, ain't I gorgeous
No one can compare with me.
But what she wiggles and she jiggles
Soon will turn to bubbalubber
And her admirers will surely flee.
But for now you can see her
Selling togs for Mr. Bollywogs
On the pages of "What's it?" Magazine.

SPRINGTIME

Someone's moving furniture
Up in the sky, I wonder why?
I hear the rumble, tumble, rumble
From room to room up in the sky
Oh no! They've hit a pipe
The heavenly ceiling is leaking
And they have called a plumber
But he can't come until the summer.

SINGING PIG

Let me sing you a song
Of fields and barnyard
Of turnips and melons
Things to chomp on.
How glorious is piggyness
And rolling in the mud.

SIC TRANSIT GLORIA MUNDI

Gloria's bus was sick on Munday
Because Munday was a Holy Day
And she didn't really want to go
To her job as a Latinish translator.
So passes the glory of the world.
Which was fine with Gloria
Because the glory of the world
Passes away with the plans of men
But Gloria couldn't care less
For the wild haired plans of men
Which in the end don't mount to much
because Mens sana in corpore sano
Most men are just happy with a clean bathroom
Idiotae viri sunt because men are idiots.

[*Latinish translation by Gloria Omnia Splendida*]

CHRISTIANITY-LITE

Oh great Tea Tray in the Sky
Bless our tea before we cry.
We do our best, we really try
Comfort us and hear our sigh.

SUNSHINE ON THE DAISIES

Sometimes his life is a jolly puzzle,
Riddle me yea, riddle me nay,
Sunshine on the daisies.

Sharp tongued Alice needs a muzzle,
Riddle me yea, riddle me nay
Sunshine on the daisies.

Old huzzy Harry is all confuzzle,
Riddle me yea, riddle me nay,
Sunshine on the daisies.

She's stirred him up with a silver swuzzle,
Riddle me yea, riddle me nay,
Sunshine on the daisies.

Until his hairy pate is all a fuzzle,
Riddle me yea, riddle me nay,
Sunshine on the daisies.

Now all his thoughts are fuzzle wuzzle,
Riddle me yea, riddle me nay,
Sunshine on the daisies.

THE CIRCUS BEAR

Now old Gumby Bear sings his song
As he jumps and dances along,
Once he rode around and around
In the center ring without a sound
As he rode his little unicycle
Now he owns his own motorcycle.
He's quit the circus and now he's free
And he hopes the same for you and me.

THE IMMEMORIAL AGE

Some say this is not the immemorial age
Of fantasy; no wisps of smoke, no ivory turrets,
No crabbéd dwarf, no lumbering troll.
Beneath their bridge the faerie light is dark
The inexplicable explained, if only outwardly.

The crabbéd dwarf still walks by my mental elven bridge
Where waits the troll, Ein pfennig, ein pfennig,
Still laughs the gnome, ein pfennig, ein pfennig,
Still wisps the smoke around the bone white turrets
Some still live what others have forgotten.

THE DUCK AND THE KING

It's a funny old thing
Said the duck to the king
With a quack and a squawk.
"Let's have a little talk
While we take a little walk
Beneath the silvery moon."
"Well ring a ding ding" said the king
"That sounds like a splendid thing."
So they walked and they talked,
The king talked and the duck squawked
All in the merry month of June.
Friendship is a wonderful thing,
Even if one is a duck and one is a king.
Friendship makes the heart go ring a ding ding.

THERE'S A BODY IN THE WELL

Who put Melvin in the well
Halfway down to hell?
There's no water in the well
But there's plenty of flames in hell.
Melvin thinks it isn't very fair
For the devil to give him such a scare.
He's had seventy strokes on the bell,
But for seventy years of sin,
It's really very fair.

FAITH AND CONTEMPLATION

A CONTEMPLATION
WATER WALKING

He came walking on the waters of the sea,
I know, for I gayly walked behind him.
There is something quite exhilarating
About walking on the surface of the sea.
The two of us were joyfully singing
Praises to the Father with a lofty hymn.
When in the distance we saw the little boat
Heaving, upon the roiling surface of the sea.
All the disciples were fiercely bailing
To keep the storm tossed craft afloat
But as we came water walking near
They cried out in panic and in great fear.
But answering He cried, out "It is I,
Do not be afraid" and calmed the sea.

AH, HOLY SPIRIT, HOLY FIRE

Ah, Holy Spirit, Holy Fire
You stir our hearts with eager fire,
You stir our minds with ardent desire.
Pour Yourself out Your people now,
Who under the turmoil of the world do bow.

Ah, Holy Spirit, Holy Fire
Behold your people now in great distress
Lest they from the pressure of the world regress.
Stir them up, pour for your Holy Fire
Stir them up with Holy desire.

Ah, Holy Spirit, Holy Fire
You stir our hearts with eager fire,
You stir our minds with ardent desire.
Pour Yourself out Your people now,
Who under the turmoil of the world do bow.

ALL TIMES ARE WAR TIMES

All times are war times
From the day when Cain killed Abel
Down to the present day.
There has always been a battle
Between the wicked and the good,
There is nothing new under the sun.
The only abiding question is
Which side are you on?
We all have two choices,
Both have eternal consequences.
There is no middle ground!
Answer the stirring trumpet call
Of wickedness that sounds out
Over this land and every land,
Or take up the bright armour of righteousness
And enlist with the saints of God.
The way of the world ends in flames
But the way of the Lord leads to that life
That celebrates in the land of eternal peace.

ENSIGN KIYOSHI OGAWA

Ensign Kiyoshi Ogawa
Rode the divine wind down
Into everlasting fire.
Hell has a way of calling
Its children home.
Violent men and women
Will discover this.

SUNSHINE AND SHADOWS

Sunshine and shadows,
A visual tapestry
Of flickering light.

THE SUN WARMED SUMMER GARDEN

In the sun warmed summer garden
The fragrance of rosemary
Fills the air, carrying
Distant hints of our lost Eden
Yet whispering, do not despair, do not despair.

THERE SHE SITS IN THE PEW

There she sits in the pew
Fleshy, radiating pheromones
Scantily clad, dripping sex
With a cold stay away face.
In the same pew a man sits
Quartered away from her.
He came to worship, but not her.

AT FOUR IN THE MORNING

"Ring out your joy to the Lord,
For praise is fitting for loyal hearts."
Whom shall I have in the morning hours
When the internal bells of Vigil ring,
But Thee O Lord, my God and my Savior?
I know that Thou lovest me!
The clamoring voices of yesterday,
The yammering voices of tomorrow,
All are silent before Thee in the Vigil hour.
All of our times are in your hand.
Yesterday is carried far away, and
Tomorrow is only a hope, not a promise.
All of our times are in your hand
All of the world waiteth upon Thee,
In the Vigil hour at four in the morning.

BATTLE CRY

There are times when the battle
Is fierce, shields clang, swords bite.
Then the sun sets, quiet descends,
A brief respite, battle's end.

By sparkling embers warriors sit
Gathered round their mighty Chief,
King of kings, Lord of Lords,
Nail prints on his hands, nail prints on his feet.

The sharp sword of truth is at his side,
From his radiant eyes. nothing hides.
When morning comes, he will call us
With the trumpet call, for this day's battle

For the moment, a brief respite.
Skirmishes tomorrow, sometimes joy,
Sometimes sorrow, sometimes losses,
Sometimes victories; until the final battle.

BITTER SWORDS

All times are war times
Ever since Cain killed Abel.

Bitter swords
And warrior shields
Men lie dying
On stony fields
Women are sighing
For husbands and sons
A lost generation.
O, blood washed fields.

Christ Jesus came to make us
His warriors and redeem us all.

BEFORE THE PASSING
OF THE PEACE

Delicious,
At least beholding her back;
Her cranberry silk dress
Falling softly from her shoulders,
Slightly gathering around her waist,
Lightly touching the shapely swell of her behind,
Cascading towards her sleek brown leather boots.

She turns slowly and I wait with anticipation.
Mutton dressed as lamb? No!
The ivory bone of her jaw,
The hollow eye sockets
Encircle an inner darkness,
Black as pitch, infinite in depth.
With a lipless smile she beckons me.
I turn and flee.

BLESSED ART THOU LORD GOD

Blesséd art Thou Lord God of the silences
When all the world lies hushed and the heart is still,
When the weary soul has given up its will
And the busy mind has lowered its defenses.

Blesséd art Thou Lord God of the dewlapp'd morning
When the lark trills his joy to the golden sun
That leaps exultant his daily course to run
While the meadows and the trees break forth singing.

Blesséd art Thou Lord God of each breaking day
When your whispering voice thunders forth your love
To all who are open to your descending Dove;
Who recognize your voice and gladly pray.

Blesséd art Thou Lord God my heavenly King
As the world awakes, to Thee with joy I sing.

COMMUNION

By circle round,
Old hand tough,
Young hands rough
Join gently round.
An old saint sways,
And smiles seraphically
With glowing marbled eyes.
Round and round
Hands meld men,
Hands meld God.

DRIVING IN THE FOG

One morning
We drove to God
In a heavy fog
The shadow lands
Pressing upon us.
The encroaching spell,
An enchantment
Of wickedness,
Was pressing upon us.
A prayer driven wind
Scattered the fog
Leaving the bare bones
Of the land visible to sight.
Pray for the travelers
Who pray for the fog
To begin once more
For they do not want
Their sins to be seen.
Lord have mercy upon us.
Lord have mercy upon them.
Lord have mercy upon us,
And let your light shine.

EVERY DAY THERE IS A CHOICE

Every day there is a choice
Between the good and evil thing
An opportunity to give voice,
And lift your voice and sing,
Or stir the anger deep within
By looking for a cause for rage,
As though it were no sin
Why pleasure in pointless outrage?
The first choice brings eternal life
The second choice ends in flames.

FAMILY APPLEYARD

In the quiet parish graveyard
Buried under holy sod
Lies the family Appleyard
Abandoned by each other,
But not hidden from their God.
Warriors all, every single one
They had a common enemy
Each one his other brother.
To whom they quite joyfully
Offered no true clemency.
Now they faced a new enemy
The God of all true unity,
Who saw with true clarity
Each blow they struck each other.
But both my Lord and I know
That preaching repentance in love
Doesn't always feel like good news.

GOSSAMER VEILS

Gossamer veils, gossamer veils,
Come dance to the tune of the gossamer veils.
Thy way is all fraught with gossamer veils,
The moon is all blood and the sky is all black,
The waning sun's robed in an old gunny sack.
Gossamer veils, gossamer veils.
There is smoke in the air near the old dragon's lair,
And the sound of his shrieking pierces the air.
The time has nigh come for the veils to be torn,
The Day of the Lord springs forth like the morn.
Gossamer veils, gossamer veils.
Nothing can hide the grim clash of the angels.
Michael and Gabriel, Raphael and Raguel,
Dance to the tune of the gossamer veils,
Uriel and Ramiel, and cold Sariel,
The host of God's angels, and many more,
They cast bright Lucifer upon the sweet earth.
For Satan, old worm, it's the end of all mirth.
Gossamer veils, gossamer veils,
Nothing protects us but gossamer veils,
Let us all dance to the gossamer veils,
Gossamer veils, gossamer veils.

HUSH NOW: A TRIALOGUE

I'm sorry, Lord, I'm sorry,
Forgive, Lord, forgive.
Hush now, you are forgiven.
I'm sorry, Lord, I'm sorry.
Hush now, you were forgiven
The very first time you asked.
He sinned, look, he sinned,
It was horrible, he sinned.
Hush now, remember
Why I threw you out of heaven.
But he sinned a terrible sin.
Hush now. I shed my blood,
His sins are washed away.
Damn, I wished to damn him.
Silence! He's mine! Silence!
My blood has washed away his sins.

IN THE HOLY PLACE

In the Holy Place,
In the midst of the saints,
We seek the face of God
Kneeling in frankincense and awe.
The soldier, the sailor,
The butcher, the baker,
The mechanic, the farmer,
The computer technician,
The wife and the husband,
Big and small, black and white,
Sinners all, each like the other,
No two stories alike,
No hearts unlike the other,
In tune, out of tune,
Belonging to one another.
The kneeling Church,
Welcomes the imperfect.
We are what we are,
God loves and transforms us.

JOY COMES EARLY IN THE MORNING

Joy comes early in the morning
With the sound of sweet birds singing
Harken to the heavenly melody
Singing praises to our heavenly Lady
Join the chorus, sing it now
With all creation, make a bow
To Mary the sweet mother
Of Him who is greater than all other.
Heaven and earth rejoice together
Singing in all kinds of weather
To the Father, to the Spirit, to the Son,
Who for us the victory has won.
Over the gates of death and hell
Ring out loudly on salvation's bell.

LESLIE THROUGH THE GOLDEN GATE

I slept I thought, and woke I knew not where
and stood before a garden wall, with birdsong in the air.
Lofty the garden wall, loftier still a golden bough
giving promise of an orchard rare.

A door was there in welcome thrown wide.
A cobbled pathway led me to the other side.
Should I dare? Should I dare to trod
within the garden of our God?

I squared my shoulders as I oft I'd done before,
and stepped I boldly through that marvelous door.
Then much to my delight, one came bounding into sight
Sophie, my old dog, leaping in the morning light.

"Allo, sweetheart," I cried with joy.
"Allo," said she, "'ows my lovely boy?
In wonder I looked down, the years had dropped away.
My dog was now a pup, and I a lovely boy.

Soft the footfalls on the garden path,
One drew near as I looked up.
O how I sought Him through the weary world,
but found Him in the breaking of the bread,
and in the lifting of the cup.

LITTLE OLD WARRIOR LADY

Little old warrior lady sitting in the pew,
Some of her memories are a little shady.
Her friends have dwindled to just a few,
But she is God's fierce warrior still.
With a bright eye for beauty, truth and love
She lifts those she loves to heaven above.
Of life's battles and losses, she has had her fill
Knocking off her rough edges, and opening her to love
Giving her prayers a clarity, born from heaven above.

OH BE JOYFUL

Oh Be Joyful
Was a miserable sod
Who spent his life
Trying to avoid his God.
But God is a patient God
And chased Oh Be Joyful
Wherever he fled
Up hill, down hill,
All along the way
Until at last Oh Be Joyful
Gave up with a shrug.
And God proclaimed his Word
"All I want is a hug!
Won't you hug me
Oh Be Joyful?"
Then Oh Be Joyful said
"Sure enough, but that's
Only the beginning."
But God said,
"A hug is a wonderful beginning,
The second thing that I want,
Is for you to be Oh Be Joyful.

OLD APPLE TREE

Old apple tree
Old apple tree
That tempted
Eve and Adam
Laying waste
The dreams of men.

Old apple tree
Old apple tree
Hewn by the axe
And rent two
To make a cross
The instrument of death.

Old apple tree
Old apple tree
Blood red your fruit
The body and the blood,
God's Son, Christ Jesus
Who died for you and me.

Old apple tree
Old apple tree
Lift high your boughs
And rejoice with us,
Christ Jesus has risen
To redeem us all.

OH TO BE WITH YOU

Oh to be with You in the midnight hours
When all is dark within, without.
Oh to be with You in a place of peace.
You are my heaven, my all right place,
You are my shelter in the midst of storm.
Life in the daylight hours spins around
With dizzying pace, sun rise, sun set,
And you are here with me within, without.
How small, how petty all the daily trials
When at night I rest myself in Thee,
You are my heaven in the midst of strife
You are my heaven in the midst of life,
You are my heavenly lover and my King,
My resting place in the midst of storm.

TARRY NOW MY LORD
AWHILE WITH ME

Tarry now my Lord awhile with me, in
The midnight hours when all is dark within
And silent spins Your wide world all around,
The ticking, chiming, clock its only sound.
There is no hiding place, dark is light to you.
No midnight fears are truly fears when you
Stretch forth your loving Spirit and enter in
Quietly cleansing, covering, healing, every sin.
From the fear of the enemy you preserve, my
Soul; in the dark You enfold and comfort me
Bringing peace, bringing calm, that I may know
That you are within, around, above, below,
Defending me as the apple of your eye.
Your freely given grace possessing me.

THE BELLS, THE BELLS

The Bells, The Bells
The sound of the bells,
the bells, the bells, the bells,
storming down the wind from the tower
of the old Cathedral on the hill.
The bells, the bells, the bells,
High tones, low tones,
ringing in the middle,
sounding out glad tidings
Christ is born again
in the hearts of grateful men.
The bells, the bells, the bells,
ringing the days of our lives,
our births, our deaths, our holy days;
the weddings of husbands and wives.
The bells, the bells, the bells,
Thirty-nine mournful strokes
Count them one by one.
Thirty-nine joyful strokes,
count them one by one,
one for you and one for all,
the toll of our redemption.
One for the Father, one for the Spirit,
and one for the Almighty Son.
The bells, the bells, the bells.
Hear them ringing down the hill.

THE CHURCH YARD OF THE REDEEMED

Down the lane and through the gate
There is a field of upright stones
And on each stone there is a name
Each name carved with infinite care
Here lies Harry, he was a liar,
And next to Harry, there lies Jane
She was crazy, quite insane.
And down the field lies Morris
Not the cat, but the Undertaker,
Alongside of his many friends.
Then there is William the wise
Not that that made any difference.
And here lies witless Wilberforce
The slow but faithful gravedigger.
He dug the graves for all of them.
But here's the secret, make it known
None of them lies buried in the grave
As penitents they shared one central thing.
Christ died for them, there is no sting.
They have risen from the dead
With Jesus who came to save.

THE CLOCK IS CHIMING FOUR

In the middle of the night
The clock is chiming four,
One for the butcher,
One for the baker,
One for the candle stick maker,
One for the village priest
Singing Vigil by the Chancel door.
The butcher is fast asleep,
The baker is firing up his ovens,
The candlestick maker is sweeping the floor
And all the while the village priest
Is singing, "Glory be to the Father!
Come morning light the butcher
Is frying bacon, giving thanks
That there is now no condemnation
For them that are in Christ Jesus.
The baker is bringing bread
Hot and fragrant from the oven
With praises for our heavenly King.
The candle stick maker is lighting
A candle in honour of Our Lady,
The village priest is singing
"Alleluia! to the Father, and to the Son,
And to the Holy Ghost."

THE UNFORGIVING CURATE

"Everything is tickety boo," said the Curate,
"Everything's alright, nothing's wrong,"
He poured the tea, "one lump or two my dear."
He smiled benignly and stirred his tea.
"It can't be all that bad my dear,
God's a generous God and not a grump,
He wouldn't hold anything against you!
Anyway, confession's not my thing, and
Anyway, absolution's not really necessary.
Did you want milk in your tea my dear?
A change of venue is what you need,
A movie, or a play, a book or a dance.
Don't worry, everything's tickety boo,
It works for me, it should work for you.

THE VANISHING BAG

I had a very painful memory
But I put it in the vanishing bag.
The bag is a magical bag.
As soon as you stow away
A memory, it begins to shrink,
But if you pull out the memory
It begins to grow and stink.
I had a high priced shrink
Who didn't understand the bag
And kept pulling out the memory
Until It grew, and I began to shrink.
Never fondle a painful memory
Acknowledge it, and put it in the bag.

IN DAYS OF DEATH AND POETRY AND AWE

In days of death and poetry and awe,
Not in the flesh but in the soul I saw
A scaly thing clutch the dying as he fell
With shrieking curse, midst stench and brimstone smell.
It's course was rudely stopped by golden wing.
The man sprang free and soaring rose on high.
The roaring demon fell earthward with a cry,
The man released from bonds began to sing.
Christ's blood had interposed and set him free,
That gracious blood was shed for you and me.
Released from shadowlands we will be,
To stand in light beside a golden sea,
And walk in flesh upon a golden shore,
And with our King rejoice for evermore.

MARY'S SONG

It was unexpected.
The angel appeared out of thin air
     radiant of face and radiant of hair,
     voice rumbling, deep waters unto deep,
     words enough to make a woman weep
         and I was but a child.
What words were they?
     "Behold you shall conceive,
     Mary maiden meek and mild."
I knew not that I was meek and mild.
I knew only consternation.
     Jesus, bone of bones,
     flesh of flesh, future King of kings.
     Before him every knee shall bow,
     every land and tongue and nation.
I could have pled my age.
I could have simply said him "No!
Not me! I am not ready! Choose another!"
I did the very thing He knew I would,
     and all my being cried out with one accord,
     Let it be to me according to your Word!
And so the deal was struck, the covenant was made
between the angel and our God, and me a little maid.

JOSEPH'S SONG

As a carpenter one thing I've seen
You can't trust the wood when it is green.
It bends and it warps 'neath the carpenters will.
A man that is green is unsteadier still.
It's been years since my own father died
Years before then I worked at his side.
Through passage of years my soul is well tried.

But what should I make of so great a tale
As large as old Jonah swallowing the whale?
She says there is no father, that there is no other.
That the Child she bears is King above all other!
She is but young, I would not shame her
But secretly would I for safety send her
Back to Judah, back to old Elizabeth
and back to older Zechariah.

That much was clear when I lay down to sleep.
In truth it was enough to make me weep.
But an angel appeared in a dream that night
His garments all glistering, radiant in light.
"Fear not to take to thee Mary as wife
The Child that she bears is the Author of Life.
Jesus, your Savior, Emmanuel King."
It's been years since my own father died
Through passage of years my soul is well tried.
I woke with my mind full of sweet light
And did what the angel bid me that night.

GLORIA

Gloria!
Birth moans
in strawed stable.
The King has come,
his lusty wailing
rends dark night.

Gloria!
Birth bloody
as his death,
the King has come.
His reality
mouth and mother's breast.

Gloria!
Birth starlit in musked air,
The King has come,
God swaddled in human need.
Gloria!
Jesus Son of God Most High.
Gloria in Excelsis Deo!
Gloria!

LADY LAUD YOUR SON

Lady laud your son.
Cast down your golden crown and worship him,
born a babe in stable laid,
who walked the hills of Galilee
with fisher folk and tax collectors
made of them a warrior band,
shocked the scribe and Pharisee
not less than priest and Sadducee.
No simple man, nor plain was he.
He has the power to call forth you and me.

Lady laud your son
whose death pierced your own soul
with grief too sharp to bear
fulfilling prophet's words in temple court
so long ago. Proud mother of a little babe
with head bowed down,
you contemplate the way
he cast down the mighty from their thrones.

Lady laud your son.
You have given once again
as you have given many times before.
Resurrection joy, ascension parting mingled in your breast.
The old ways of holding him can never be again.
Lady laud your son.
Cast down your golden crown and worship him
in the circle of the saints, his sisters, brothers,
all your children now, all crowned like you
God-bearer, now for ever blessed
held in warm embrace by glad hearts everywhere.
Lady laud your son.

WHEN LOVE IS BORN
AT CHRISTMAS

When love is born at Christmas
the busy world is hushed,
all creation waits to hear
the infant's cry of life.

The sheep and oxen gather
'round the humble manger,
The young mother kneels to see
God's holy Child, now hers.

God Himself is bending there,
Yielding self to human care,
To Mary humble mother
and to Joseph standing there.

In the fields not far away
Shepherds guard their flocks by night,
When all the heavens shine bright
With angels in brilliant light,

Singing loud Alleluias,
Jesus, God's Son, is born tonight.
Let no evil you affright,
He comes to set things right.

And what do these shepherds see?
A baby in a manger,
such a simple thing to see;
with his mother Mary kneeling by.

THE WINDING CENTURIES
HAVE COME AND GONE

The winding centuries have come and gone
Still the Christmas song goes on and on.
Some have loved the Babe, some still hate him;
Christmas joy is for hearts that welcome him.
Peace on earth, the thronging angels sing,
Throughout the heavens hear the merry chorus ring.
Simple shepherds on the hill rejoice to hear
The news that Almighty God has drawn near.
But Herod on his throne feels a deadly chill;
Any who threaten his power he will kill,
Wife, or son, or even little baby child.
There is no safety for child or mother mild.
Now Herod is dead; the years have come and gone;
Only Christ will come with the breaking of the dawn.

GOD'S GIFT OF GLORY BRIGHT

Behold a great light in the darkness shining, God's gift of glory
bright, Jesus, Light of Light.
Once in glory dwelling, now in flesh abiding,
Jesus, God's gift of love, born for you and me.

Refrain
Mary has a baby, our Emmanuel.
Jesus, Son of God, born for you and me.

Little Son of God in a manger lying,
Joseph, Angels, shepherds, sheep and oxen praising,
Mary's tiny babe, in the stable dwelling.
Jesus King of Kings, Lord of all we see.

Refrain
Mary has a baby, our Emmanuel.
Jesus, Son of God, born for you and me.

OUR CHRISTMAS HEARTS
ARE CAROLING

Our Christmas hearts are caroling
that love is born our heavenly King.

The cold world wounds, its raw winds roar,
with this heavenly child our hearts will soar.

In the infant's smile and the infants tear
we'll find the peace that quells our fear.

He came the lives of men to share
the cross to bear and the pain to bear.

Though men will suffer, men will die
God's children know that he is nigh.

Our Christmas hearts are caroling
that love is born our heavenly king.

Printed in the United States
By Bookmasters